BLAST OFF!
NEPTUNE

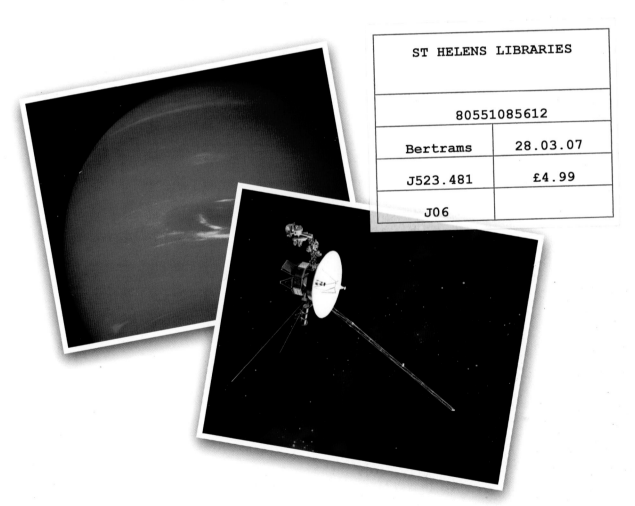

Helen and David Orme

Copyright © ticktock Entertainment Ltd 2007
First published in Great Britain in 2006 by ticktock Media Ltd.,
Unit 2, Orchard Business Centre, North Farm Road,
Tunbridge Wells, Kent, TN2 3XF

ticktock project editor: Julia Adams
ticktock project designer: Emma Randall

We would like to thank: Sandra Voss, Tim Bones, James Powell,
Indexing Specialists (UK) Ltd.

ISBN 978 1 84696 055 0
Printed in China
A CIP catalogue record for this book is available from the British Library.

Picture credits
t=top, b=bottom, c=centre, l-left, r=right, bg=background
Sam Chavan: 15tr; Hubble Space Telescope: 18, 19; NASA: front cover, 1 all, 6tr, 7t, 8, 9c, 11tl, 11tr, 15bl, 17tl, 20 all, 22, 23;
Science Photo Library: 4/5bg (original), 13, 14, 21; Shutterstock: 2/3bg, 6tl, 9bl, 17br, 24bg; ticktock picture archive: 5, 6/7bg,
6b, 7b, 9t, 10/11bg, 10, 11b, 12, 14/15bg, 16, 18/19bg, 22/23bg;
Every effort has been made to trace the copyright holders, and we apologise in advance for any unintentional omissions.
We would be pleased to insert the appropriate acknowledgements in any subsequent edition of this publication.

Contents

Where is Neptune?

There are eight planets in our **solar system**. The planets travel around the Sun. Neptune is the furthest planet from the Sun.

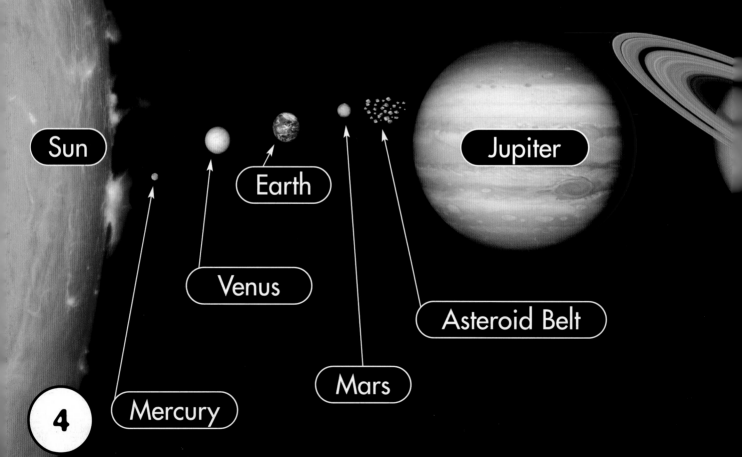

Sun

Mercury

Venus

Earth

Mars

Asteroid Belt

Jupiter

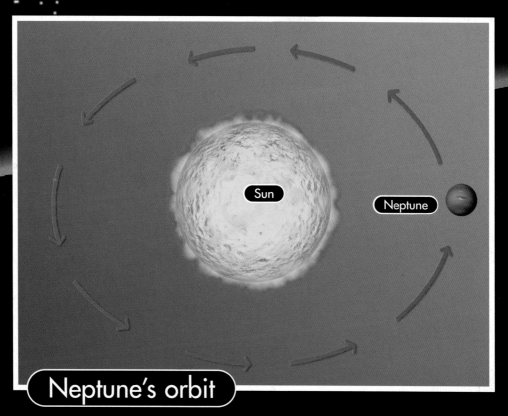

Neptune's orbit

Neptune travels around the Sun once every 165 **Earth years**. This journey is called its **orbit**. The time it takes for a planet to travel around the Sun once is called a **year**.

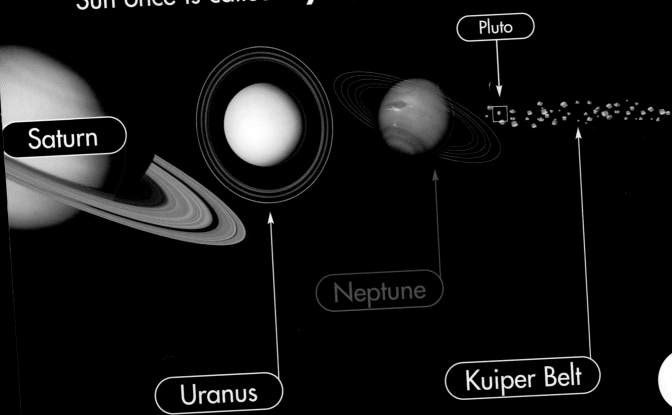

Saturn

Uranus

Neptune

Pluto

Kuiper Belt

Neptune is the fourth biggest planet in the **solar system**. About 60 Earths could fit inside Neptune!

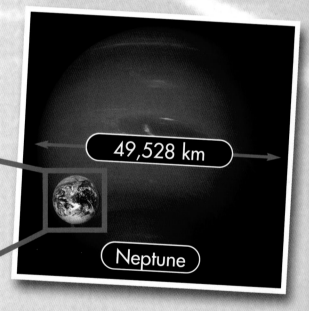

49,528 km

12,756 km

Earth

Neptune

inside Neptune

Neptune has an **atmosphere** of gases.

Below the atmosphere is a mixture of water, ices and gases.

The centre might be made of rock and ice.

Planets are always spinning. The time it takes a planet to spin around once is called a **day**. One day on Neptune is the same as 16 hours on Earth.

Sometimes Neptune is further away from the Sun than the **dwarf planet** Pluto. This happens when Pluto's **orbit** brings it closer to the Sun than Neptune.

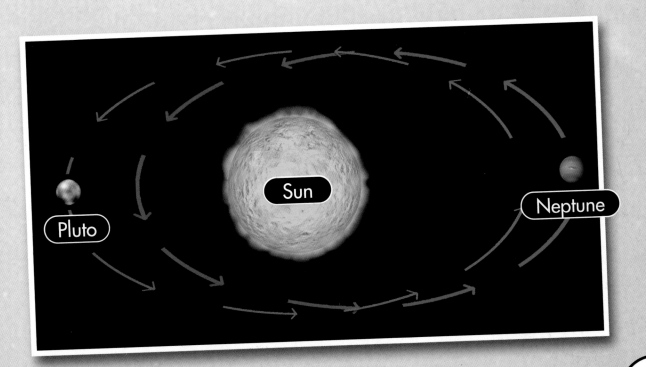

Sun

Pluto

Neptune

This will not happen again for about another 230 years!

The fastest winds in the **solar system** roar around Neptune at up to 2092 kilometres an hour! The fastest winds ever recorded on Earth were 350 km an hour.

These photographs of Neptune show clouds and bands of wind. They were taken by telescopes on Earth and by the **Hubble Space Telescope**.

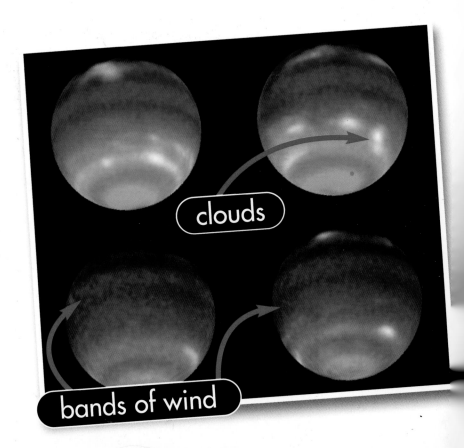

clouds

bands of wind

atmosphere

Neptune looks blue because of the **methane gas** in the planet's **atmosphere**.

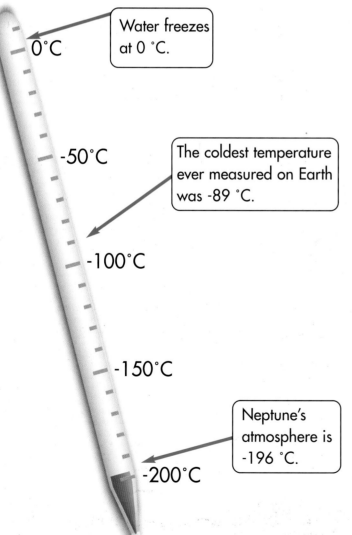

Water freezes at 0 °C.

0°C

-50°C

The coldest temperature ever measured on Earth was -89 °C.

-100°C

-150°C

Neptune's atmosphere is -196 °C.

-200°C

Great Dark Spot

This is the Great Dark Spot, a storm as big as our Earth! This photograph was taken by the Voyager 2 **space probe** in 1989.

Neptune's Moons

Neptune has 13 moons that we know about. Our Earth only has one!
The painting on this page shows three small moons that **astronomers** discovered in 2002 and 2003.

Neptune

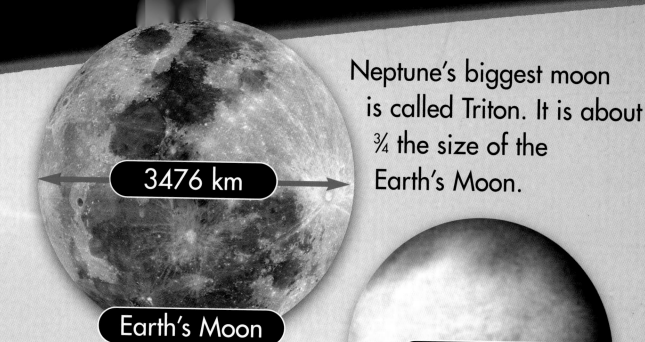

Neptune's biggest moon is called Triton. It is about ¾ the size of the Earth's Moon.

3476 km

Earth's Moon

2709 km

Triton

Neptune's moon Nereid has a very oval **orbit**. At its closest, Nereid is 816,568 km from Neptune. But at its furthest, it is nearly 9 ½ million km from the planet!

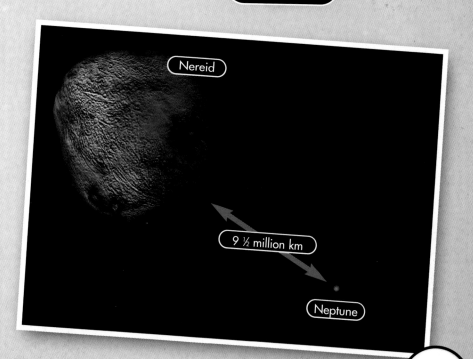

Nereid

9 ½ million km

Neptune

Triton

Triton is the coldest place in the **solar system**. The temperature on this moon is about -240 °C.

Scientists think that Triton did not form at the same time as Neptune.

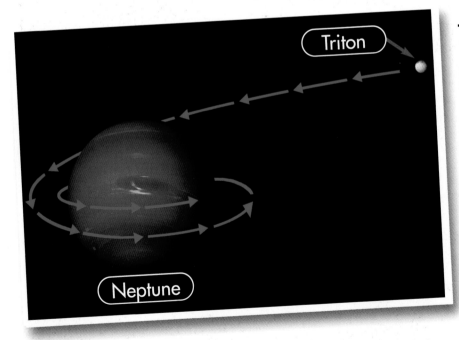

Triton

Neptune

Triton was probably moving through space when Neptune pulled this moon into **orbit** around it.

Triton is slowly getting closer to Neptune. It will probably crash into the planet in about 3 billion years.

Triton has **geysers**.
They shoot icy gases and dust into the air.
This material freezes and falls back down
onto Triton like snow.

Gases from a geyser being blown by strong winds

Neptune

A painting of Triton

Voyager 2 spotted one geyser shooting
gases and ice 8 kilometres high!

Neptune's Rings

Neptune has five complete rings. The rings are probably made of rocks and dust.

Neptune's neighbours Uranus and Saturn have rings, too. When these were discovered, **astronomers** guessed that Neptune might have rings.

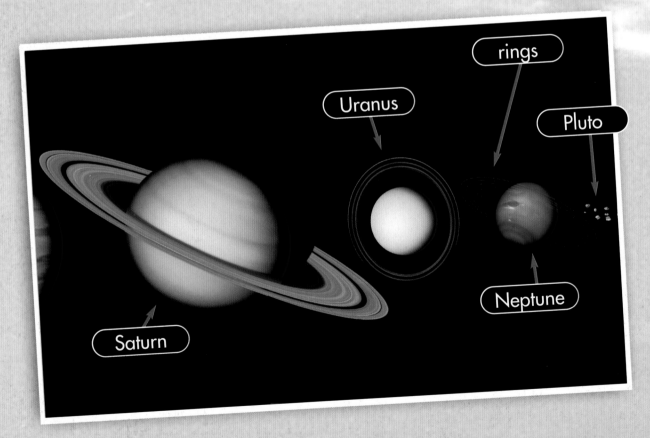

rings

Uranus

Pluto

Saturn

Neptune

No one knew for sure until the **space probe** Voyager 2 discovered the rings in 1989.

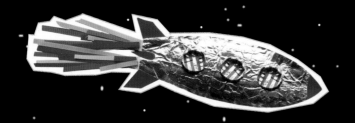

Scientists think that when rocks hit Neptune's moons, dust and bits of rock fly off into space. The dust and rocks are added to the planet's rings.

A painting of Neptune's rings

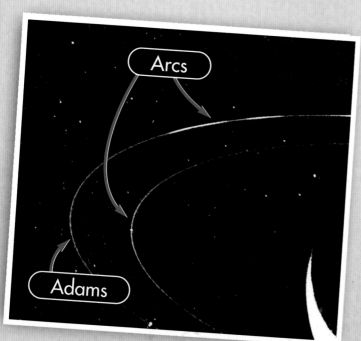

Arcs

Adams

This photograph from Voyager 2 shows the outer ring. It is called Adams.

The ring is thicker in some places than others. The thicker places are called arcs.

Neptune was first identified by the German astronomer Johann Galle in 1846.

Johann Galle

Before Galle discovered Neptune, its position in space had already been figured out. The French scientist Urbain Joseph Le Verrier and the English astronomer John Adams used mathematics to guess where Neptune was.

Neptune

Johann Galle used Le Verrier's maths to work out where to look in the sky. He discovered Neptune in 1846.

Because it looks blue, the new planet was named after Neptune, the ancient Roman god of the sea.

The moon Triton was named after Neptune's son.

A statue of Neptune

What Can We See?

It is impossible to see Neptune without using a telescope, because it is so far from the Earth.

The best pictures of Neptune come from the **Hubble Space Telescope**. This telescope **orbits** the Earth out in space.

Hubble is 568 km above Earth's surface.

Because Hubble is outside of the Earth's **atmosphere**, its pictures are much clearer than pictures from even the biggest telescopes on Earth.

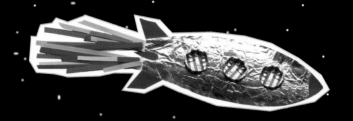

These pictures,
taken by Hubble, show springtime
on the southern half of Neptune. They show the bands
of clouds getting lighter in the south. This is a sign of
the Sun warming up this part of Neptune.

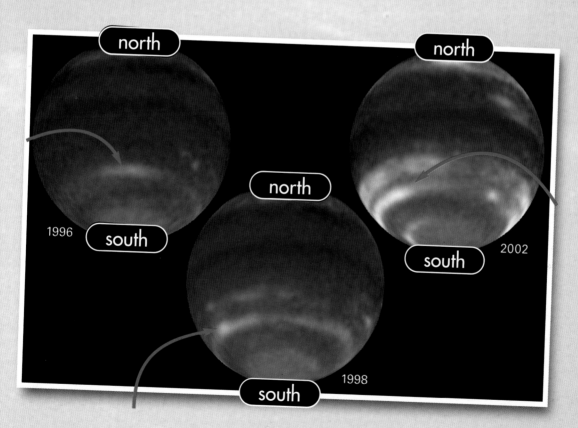

north

north

1996

south

north

south

2002

1998

south

Because a year on Neptune lasts for
165 **Earth years**, springtime on Neptune
lasts for about 40 Earth years!

Missions to Neptune

Voyager 2 is the only space mission there has been to Neptune. The Voyager 2 **space probe** discovered Neptune's rings and some of its moons.

Voyager 2 blasted into space aboard a Titan-Centaur rocket on 20th August, 1977.

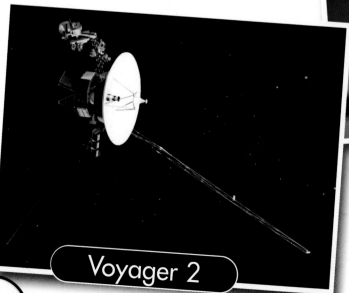

Titan-Centaur rocket

Voyager 2

Voyager 2 travelled first to Jupiter, Saturn, and Uranus. It finally reached Neptune in 1989.

Voyager 2 measured the temperature on Neptune and the speed of the wind on the planet.

Sun

Voyager 2

Neptune

Voyager 2 is now moving towards the edge of our **solar system**. Scientists hope it will send information back to Earth until 2030.

Future Missions

NASA is planning a new mission to Neptune and its moons. If it goes ahead, the mission will be launched between 2016 and 2018. The spacecraft for this mission will arrive at Neptune in 2035!

Triton

The spacecraft will send two **landers** to Triton's surface.

In addition, **space probes** will be sent into Neptune's **atmosphere**.

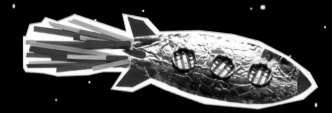

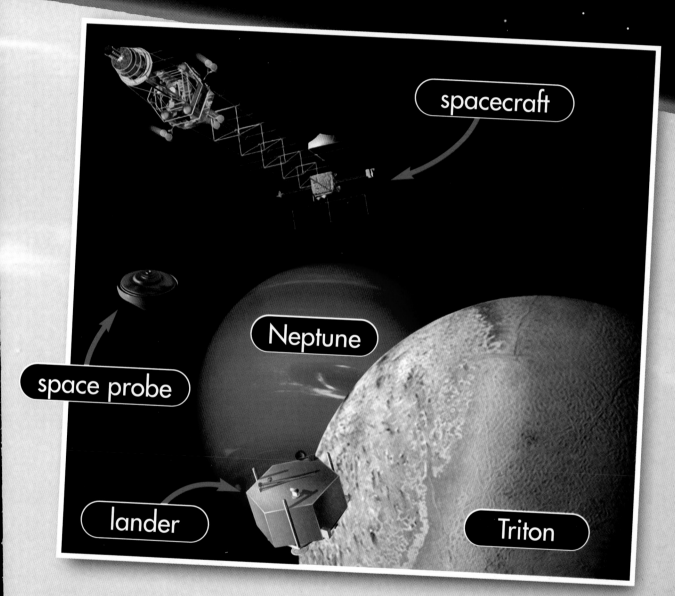

spacecraft

Neptune

space probe

lander

Triton

Neptune and Triton are very old. They haven't changed much since they were formed. Studying them might give us new information about how the **solar system** was formed.

Glossary

Astronomers People who study space, often using telescopes.

Atmosphere The gases that surround a star, planet or moon.

Day A day is the time it takes a planet to spin around once. A day on Earth is 24 hours long.

Earth years A year is the time it takes for a planet to orbit the Sun. An Earth year is 365 days long.

Dwarf planet An object smaller than a planet that orbits around the Sun.

Geysers A place on the surface of a planet or a moon, where gases, ice and water shoot into the air from time to time.

Hubble Space Telescope A telescope that orbits the Earth. Its pictures of space are very clear because it is outside of Earth's atmosphere.

Landers Spacecraft designed to land on a planet or moon.

Methane gas A gas with no smell. It burns easily.

NASA (short for National Aeronautics and Space Administration) An American group of scientists and astronomers who research space.

Orbit The path that a planet or other object takes around the Sun, or a satellite takes around a planet.

Solar system The Sun and everything that is in orbit around it.

Space probe A spacecraft sent from Earth to explore the solar system. It can collect samples and take pictures.

Year The time it takes for a planet to orbit the Sun once.

Index